Text by Lois Rock
Illustrations copyright © 2008 Sophie Allsopp
This edition copyright © 2013 Lion Hudson

Published by Lion Children's Books
an imprint of
Lion Hudson plc
Wilkinson House, Jordan Hill Road,
Oxford OX2 8DR, England
www.lionhudson.com/lionchildrens
ISBN 978 0 7459 6320 4

First edition 2008
This edition 2013

A catalogue record for this book is available from the British Library

Printed and bound in China, November 2012, LH17

The First
EASTER

Lois Rock

Illustrated by Sophie Allsopp

LION
CHILDREN'S

Long ago there lived a man named Jesus.
  He was a storyteller and a miracle worker and a preacher.
  "And he tells us the good news," said the children, "that God loves us."

One spring day, Jesus
spoke to his twelve disciples.

"It's festival time," he said, "and we should go to
the Temple in Jerusalem for the celebrations."

When the crowds saw Jesus riding to the city,
they began to whisper:

"Perhaps Jesus is going to make himself our king!
Perhaps that is how he will make us all God's people."

They began to cheer and to wave palm branches.

But Jesus did not say anything about being a king.
He simply went to the Temple.

To his dismay, the festival market was in full swing.

"This is wrong!" he cried. "The Temple is meant to be a place to say prayers to God!"

All at once, he sent the tables clattering and the people scattering.

In the quiet, dark corners the priests gathered and scowled.

"Troublemaker," they whispered. "We must get rid of him."

Jesus paid them no attention. He went on preaching about God and God's love. He still went on doing what he always did: day after day, he preached to those who would listen.

"If you truly want to be God's friends," he told his listeners, "you must do the things that are right and good."

Even as he spoke, the disciple named Judas let dark thoughts cloud his mind.

He went to the priests and whispered: "I can help you capture Jesus."

Even so, all seemed well
when Jesus and his disciples met
for the special festival meal.
Jesus took the bread and shared it with them.
"This is my body," he said. "It will be broken for you."
Then he took a cup of wine and gave it to them.
"This is my blood," he said. "It will be spilled for you. When
you meet together, eat and drink these things in memory of me."

Evening turned to night. In an olive grove called Gethsemane, the disciples fell asleep.

Jesus stayed awake praying.

He had seen Judas go off alone. He was not surprised to see him return… with a band of armed men.

The guards seized Jesus roughly.

The disciples ran away.

For Jesus there was no escape.

All through the night, the priests put together
the story they wanted to tell.

In the morning, they marched Jesus to the governor,
Pontius Pilate.

"This man claims to be a king," they told Pilate. "He's a threat
to law and order. You must have him put to death."

What they said was not true, but they got their way. Pilate gave the order to the army. "Take this Jesus and have him crucified."

The soldiers hustled Jesus out of the city.

They nailed him to a cross as if he were a criminal.

As the crowds jeered, Jesus said a prayer:

"Forgive them, Father God. They don't know what they are doing."

As the sun sank low, some of Jesus'
friends came to take the body down.
They carried it to a stone tomb.

"There's no time for the funeral customs," wept
the women. "It's nearly sunset, when the holy day
of rest begins."

Hurriedly they rolled the stone door shut and
went away.

Very early on Sunday morning, the women came back.
  They gasped in dismay.
  The tomb was open. Jesus' body had gone.
  As they stood there crying, two angels appeared.
  "Why are you looking among the dead?" asked the angels.
"Jesus is alive."

It was news beyond anything they had ever dreamed. In the days that followed, Jesus' loyal followers saw him and touched him.

"I have done everything I came to do," explained Jesus. "Now I want you to go on spreading the good news that I have told you.

"Soon I will go to be with my Father God in heaven.

"After that, God will send you all the help you need to do the task."

And so it was. One day, when Jesus' followers were together, they heard a noise like blowing wind. They saw flames of bright fire blazing above them.

They felt brave and strong as never before.
That very day they began to spread the good
news about Jesus.

The news about God's love: the love that will
last for ever.